THE CHILDREN'S BIBLE

Volume 12

A Golden Press / Funk & Wagnalls, Inc. Book
Published by Western Publishing Company, Inc.

Classic™ binding
R. R. Donnelley & Sons Company
patents--U.S. pending
Distributed by Funk & Wagnalls, Inc. New York
Library of Congress Catalog Card Number: 81-81439
ISBN 0-8343-0049-4 (Volume 12)
ISBN 0-8343-0037-0 (12 Volume Set)

CONTENTS

INTRODUCTION

Just before Jesus ascended into heaven, he gave his apostles a vitally important job to do. He told them to go out and tell the whole world that he had suffered and died for all men and women, and that he had risen from the dead to give them eternal life. He wanted the apostles to preach the good news that the world had been given a new and fresh start. Jesus wanted his apostles to spread the joyous word far and wide.

This was not an easy job for the apostles, who were poor fishermen from Galilee. They did not know how they could talk about Jesus to people who lived in faraway lands and who spoke different languages. They feared the sufferings of long voyages and the sadness of being away from home. And most frightening of all, they knew some people would hear their message and persecute them for it.

Jesus knew how difficult a job he had given the apostles. He promised his apostles that he would be with them always, and he kept his promise by sending the power of God to them in the form of the Holy Spirit. The Spirit gave the apostles the confidence to preach, enabled them to endure persecution, and taught the first missionaries what to say. The apostles were no longer unsure of themselves because they did not have to act alone. They had help now and so they were ready to tell the world about their Lord and Savior.

The Holy Spirit descended on the apostles during the feast of Pentecost. Pentecost was a Jewish holiday called the Harvest Feast, which took place seven weeks after the beginning of the barley harvest. It was a joyous holiday of thanksgiving—a time for Jews to show their gratefulness for God's many gifts to the world. The earliest Christians remained faithful to their Jewish heritage and kept traditional feast days like Pentecost. But these celebrations took on a new meaning for them because they remembered the great things Jesus had accomplished. Today Christians still celebrate the feast of Pentecost by thanking God for sending the Holy Spirit to them. They believe that the Spirit is still with them today, helping and guiding them in the modern world.

Some of the first followers of Jesus were called Nazarenes. They were Jews who believed Jesus was the Messiah, but they continued to keep the Sabbath as they had always done and they circumcised their male children. They thought of themselves as Jews with one important difference—they believed in Jesus as Lord and Savior. The first Christians were mostly poor people. They lived near each other and met often to celebrate the Eucharist. Heeding Jesus' warning that it would be difficult for the rich to enter heaven, they shared everything they owned with one another and always helped those in need. Although they were a small and poor community, these Christians were strong because they shared their faith in Jesus.

As the Christians began to preach about Jesus, men and women who were not Jewish became interested in their message. Some of these people wanted to join the Christian community. This posed a serious and difficult problem that threatened the Christians' unity. The apostles could not agree whether Gentile Christians had to observe all the Jewish customs and keep all the Jewish holidays.

The man who finally answered this question for the Christian community was Paul, a former Jew who became a great Christian missionary. He convinced the Christian leaders in Jerusalem that Christ had come to save all men and women, Jew and Gentile. Paul believed that since Christ had come, it was no longer necessary for any Christians to follow Jewish customs. What was important, Paul said, was that men and women have faith in Jesus as Lord and Messiah.

Paul himself had not always believed in Jesus. He had been trained as a Pharisee and was well educated in the law because he studied for many years in Jerusalem to be a rabbi. As a young man, Paul was one of the people who persecuted the Christians in Judea. But then he had a very special experience. We are told by Luke, who edited the Acts of the Apostles, that the risen Jesus appeared to Paul and asked him why he was persecuting his followers. This event changed Paul's whole life—he became an earnest follower of Jesus.

Paul spent the rest of his life telling all men and women about the wonderful gift of salvation that Jesus had given the world. He went on several long and difficult journeys through the Mediterranean area, because he knew that the people outside of Judea had not heard about the most important event of all time. Paul wanted the whole world to know that Jesus had died and been raised for all men and women.

Paul also wanted all Christians to live together in peace and love. In the letters he wrote to the Christian communities he visited, this great missionary taught Christians that just as they believed in one Lord, Jesus Christ, so they should live together as one community. The foundation of their lives should be their shared faith in Christ. Paul's message still challenges Christians today to live together in peace and unity.

from the
BOOKS OF ACTS,
GALATIANS, ROMANS,
CORINTHIANS and
THESSALONIANS

THE COMING OF THE HOLY SPIRIT

WHEN the day of Pentecost had come, the disciples were all gathered together in one place. And suddenly there came a sound from heaven like a rushing mighty wind, and it filled all the house where they were sitting.

And there appeared to them tongues of flame which sat upon each of them. And they were all filled with the Holy Spirit, and began to speak in other languages, as the Spirit led them to speak.

Now there were living in Jerusalem Jews, devout men, from every nation under heaven. And when this news spread, the multitude came together and were confounded because every man heard them speak in his own language.

They were all amazed and marveled, saying to one another, "Behold, are not all these who speak Galileans? How is it that each of us hears his own language from where he was born? Parthians and Medes and Elamites, and the dwellers of Mesopotamia, and of Judea and Cappadocia and Pontus and Asia, of Phrygia and Pamphylia, of Egypt and the parts of Libya around

Cyrene, and strangers from Rome, Jews and proselytes, Cretans and Arabs, we hear them speak in our own tongues of the wonderful works of God."

They were all amazed and wondered, saying to one another, "What does this mean?"

Others, mocking, said, "These men are full of new wine."

But Peter, standing up with the eleven (for they had chosen Matthias to take the place of the traitor Judas), lifted up his voice and said to them, "You men of Judea, and all you who live in Jerusalem, listen to my words and know this: These men are not drunken, as you suppose, for it is only the ninth hour of the day. But this is that which was spoken by God to the prophet Joel: 'And it shall come to pass in the last days, that I will pour out my Spirit upon all men. And your sons and your daughters shall prophesy, and your young men shall see visions and your old men shall dream dreams.' " And he told them of Jesus the Christ, the Son of God.

Then those who gladly received his word were baptized, and that same day were added to them about three thousand souls. They followed faithfully the apostles' teaching and fellowship, breaking bread together and praying.

And fear came upon every soul and many wonders were done by the apostles. All that believed were together and owned all things in common. They sold their possessions and goods and divided the money among all the people, as each had need of it.

Daily they went together to the temple, and from house to house they ate with gladness and singleness of heart, praising God and having favor with all the people. And the Lord added to their number daily those who would be saved.

715

A LAME BEGGAR HEALED

Now Peter and John went together into the temple at the hour of prayer, being the third hour of the afternoon. And a certain man, lame from birth, was laid daily at the gate of the temple which is called Beautiful, to ask alms of those who enter the temple.

Seeing Peter and John about to go into the temple, he asked alms of them. And Peter, fixing his eyes upon him, said, "Look at us." He looked at them, expecting to receive something from them. Then Peter said to him, "Silver and gold I have none, but what I have I give you. In the name of Jesus Christ of Nazareth, rise up and walk."

And he took him by the right hand and lifted him up. Immediately his feet and ankle bones received strength, and he, leaping up, stood and walked, and entered with them into the temple, walking and leaping and praising God.

The people saw him walking and heard him praising God, and they knew that it was he who had sat begging at the gate Beautiful of the temple; they were filled with amazement and wonder at what had happened to him.

When Peter saw this, he said to the people, "You men of Israel, why do you marvel at this? Why do you stare at us so, as though by our own power or holiness we have made this man walk?

"The God of Abraham and of Isaac, and of Jacob, the God of our fathers, is thus glorifying his Son, Jesus, whom you delivered up and denied in the presence of Pilate, when he was determined to let him go. But you denied the Just and Holy One, and demanded that a murderer be set free for you. You killed the Prince of life, whom God has raised from the dead. Of that we are witnesses. And his name, through faith in his name, has made this man strong whom you well know."

THE APOSTLES ARE ARRESTED

As they spoke to the people, the priests and the captain of the temple and the Sadducees came upon them and were angered that they taught the people and preached the resurrection from the dead, through Jesus. They arrested them and held them until the next day, for it was evening.

However, many of those who heard the word believed, and the number of them grew to about five thousand.

The next day, the rulers and elders and scribes, Annas the high priest, and Caiaphas, and John and Alexander and as many as were of the family of the high priest gathered together at Jerusalem.

They conferred among themselves, saying:

"What shall we do with these men? That a notable miracle was done by them is clear to all the people of Jerusalem, and we cannot deny it. But so that it spreads no further, let us threaten them, that they speak hereafter to no man in this name." And they called them, and commanded them not to speak at all nor teach in the name of Jesus.

But Peter and John answered and said to them:

"Whether it is right in the sight of God to listen more to you than to God, you judge. For we can only speak of the things which we have seen and heard."

And when they had threatened them further, they let them go, finding no way to punish them because of the people.

Then great wonders were worked among the people by the hands of the apostles, so much so that the people brought forth the sick into the streets and laid them on beds and couches so that at least the shadow of Peter passing by might fall upon some of them.

There came a multitude from the cities around Jerusalem, bringing sick folk and those who were troubled with evil spirits. And they were healed, every one.

Then the high priest rose up, and all the Sadducees who were with him, and they were filled with indignation. They laid their hands upon the apostles and put them in the common prison.

THE APOSTLES ESCAPE

But the angel of the Lord opened the prison doors by night, and brought them out, and said, "Go, stand up in the temple and speak to the people all the words of this life." And when they heard that, they went into the temple early in the morning, and taught.

Now the high priest and they that were with him called together the council and all the senate of the children of Israel, and sent to the prison to have them brought. When the officers went and did not find them in the prison, they returned, saying, "The prison we found shut securely and the keepers standing outside before the doors, but when we opened them, we found no man within."

Then someone came and told them, "Behold, the men whom you put in prison are standing in the temple and teaching the people." And when the high priest and the captain of the temple and the chief priests heard these things, they wondered what would come of them.

STEPHEN, THE FIRST MARTYR

The apostles chose seven men to help them with their daily affairs, and among these was Stephen, a man full of faith and of the Holy Spirit. He did great wonders and miracles among the people. Some members of the synagogue disputed with him, but they were not able to stand up to his wisdom and the spirit with which he spoke.

So they got some men to say, "We have heard him speak blasphemous words against Moses and against God." And they stirred up the people and the elders and the scribes, and they came upon him and seized him and brought him before the council.

They set up false witnesses who said, "This man never ceases speaking blasphemous words against this holy place and the law.

"We have heard him say that this Jesus of Nazareth shall destroy this place and shall change the customs which Moses gave us."

And all those who sat in the council looked at him, and saw that his face was like the face of an angel.

Then the high priest said, "Are these things so?"

STEPHEN MAKES HIS DEFENSE

Stephen said, "Men, brothers and fathers, listen. The Most High does not dwell in temples made with hands, for as the prophet says, 'Heaven is my throne, and the earth is my footstool. What house will you build me?' says the Lord. 'Or what is the place of my rest? Has not my hand made all these things?'

"You stubborn people, heathen in heart and heathen in hearing! You always resist the Holy Spirit. As your fathers did, so do you. Which of the prophets did not your fathers persecute? And they killed those who foretold the coming of the Just One; whom you have just now betrayed and murdered—you who received the law from the angels but have not kept it!"

When they heard these things, they were cut to the heart and ground their teeth at him. But he, being full of the Holy Spirit, looked steadily up into heaven and saw the glory of God, and Jesus standing on the right hand of God.

He said, "Behold, I see the heavens opened and the Son of man standing on the right hand of God."

Then they cried out with a loud voice, and stopped up their ears, and ran upon him all at once. They threw him out of the city and stoned him. And the witnesses laid down their cloaks at the feet of a young man whose name was Saul.

As they stoned Stephen, he called upon God, saying, "Lord Jesus, receive my spirit." He kneeled down and cried out with a loud voice, "Lord, do not count this sin against them." And when he had said this, he fell asleep in death.

SAUL IS CONVERTED

Not only did Saul consent to Stephen's death but he was directing heavy persecution against the church in Jerusalem, entering into every house and dragging out men and women to put them into prison. Breathing out threats of slaughter against the disciples of the Lord, Saul went to the high priest and asked from him letters to the synagogue in Damascus, so that if he found any who followed Christ's way, whether they were men or women, he might bring them bound to Jerusalem.

But as he journeyed, approaching Damascus, suddenly there shone around him a light from heaven, and he fell to the earth and heard a voice saying to him, "Saul, Saul, why do you persecute me?" And he said, "Who are you, Lord?" And the Lord said, "I am Jesus, whom you persecute."

Then he, trembling and astonished, said, "Lord, what do you want me to do?" And the Lord said to him,

"Arise and go into the city, and you shall be told what you must do."

The men who journeyed with him stood speechless, hearing a voice but seeing no man.

Saul arose from the earth, and when he opened his eyes, he could see no man. But they led him by the hand and brought him into Damascus. For three days he was without sight, and neither ate nor drank.

Now there was a certain disciple in Damascus named Ananias. And the Lord said to him in a vision, "Ananias." And he answered, "Yes, I am here, Lord."

The Lord said to him, "Arise and go into the street called Straight, and ask in the house of Judas for a man called Saul of Tarsus. For he is praying and has seen in a vision a man named Ananias coming in and putting his hand upon him that he might receive his sight."

Then Ananias said, "Lord, I have heard from many people about this man and how much evil he has done to your saints at Jerusalem. And here he has authority from the chief priests to arrest all that call upon your name."

But the Lord said to him, "Go your way, for he is chosen by me to carry my name to the Gentiles, and kings, and the children of Israel. For I shall show him how greatly he must suffer for my name's sake."

SAUL BECOMES A CHRISTIAN

Ananias went his way and entered the house, and putting his hands on Saul, said, "Brother Saul, the Lord, even Jesus who appeared to you on the road as you came, has sent me that you might receive your sight and be filled with the Holy Spirit."

Immediately it was as if scales fell from his eyes, and he received his sight at once, and arose and was baptized.

When he had eaten, he was stronger, and he stayed on for some days with the disciples who were in Damascus. He began preaching in the synagogues that Christ is the Son of God. And all who heard him were amazed, and said, "Is this not he who destroyed those who called on Christ's name in Jerusalem, and came here in order to bring them bound to the chief priests?"

But Saul increased all the more in strength, and confounded his foes who lived in Damascus, by proving that Jesus was indeed the Christ.

After many days had passed, they plotted to kill him. But Saul knew that they were lying in wait for him, and that they watched the gates day and night to kill him. So the disciples took him by night and let him down over the wall in a basket. And when Saul came to Jerusalem, he joined the disciples there.

THE TEACHING OF PETER

There was a certain man in Caesarea called Cornelius, a centurion of the Roman army. He was a devout man, one who feared God with all his household, who gave much alms to the people and prayed to God constantly.

on him, and when he had told them of all these things, he sent them to Joppa.

On the next day, as they went on their journey and drew near to the city, Peter went up onto the housetop for his noonday prayers. And while he was there, the men whom Corne-

He saw in a vision one afternoon an angel of God come to him and say, "Cornelius." When he looked at him, he was afraid and said, "What is it, Lord?"

And the angel said to him, "Your prayers and your alms have come up before God as a memorial. Now send men to Joppa, and call for one Simon whose other name is Peter. He is staying with one Simon, a tanner, whose house is by the seaside. He shall tell you what you ought to do."

When the angel who spoke to Cornelius had gone away, he called two of his household servants and a devout soldier from among them who waited

lius had sent, having made enquiry for Simon's house, stood before the gate. They called and asked whether Simon called Peter was staying there.

In the midst of Peter's prayers, the Holy Spirit said to him, "Behold, three men seek you. Arise therefore, go down and go with them. Do not worry about anything, for I am the one who has sent them."

Then Peter went down to the men and said, "Behold, I am the one whom you seek. Why have you come?" And they said, "Cornelius the centurion, a just man and one who fears God, a man of good reputation among the whole Jewish nation, was told by a holy angel of God to send for you to come to his house, so that he could hear you speak."

Then he called them in and gave them lodging. And the next day Peter went away with them, and certain of the brothers from Joppa went with him.

any man is unclean. Therefore I came to you without question as soon as I was sent for. I ask now for what purpose you have sent for me?"

Cornelius told him of his vision. Then Peter began to speak and said, "Truly I can see that God favors no person, but among every people he

PETER AND THE CENTURION

The following day, they entered Caesarea and Cornelius was waiting for them, having called together his kinsmen and close friends. As Peter came in, Cornelius met him and fell down at his feet and worshiped him. But Peter lifted him up, saying, "Stand up, I myself also am a man."

As they talked, he went in and found that there were many gathered together. And Peter said to them, "You know that it is an unlawful thing for a man that is a Jew to keep company or visit with anyone of another people. But God has taught me not to feel that

who fears him and does what is right is acceptable to him."

While Peter was speaking to them, the Holy Spirit fell on all those who heard his words. And all those believers among the Jews who had come with Peter were astonished because the gift of the Holy Spirit was poured out even upon the Gentiles. For they heard them speak in strange words and glorify God. Then Peter said, "Can any man deny them water to be baptized, these who have received the Holy Spirit as well as we?" And he commanded them to be baptized in the name of the Lord. They begged him to remain with them for some days.

PETER IS IMPRISONED

Now about that time, Herod the king reached out to strike certain of the followers of Christ. He had James the brother of John killed with the sword. And, because he saw it pleased the people, he proceeded further to seize Peter too.

When he had arrested him, he put him in prison and delivered him to four squads of soldiers to guard him, intending after the Passover to bring him forth to the people. So Peter was kept in prison, but the prayers of the church were made unceasingly to God for him.

When Herod was about to bring him forth, that same night Peter was sleeping between two soldiers, bound with two chains. And the keepers at the doors guarded the prison. And, behold, an angel of the Lord came to him, and a light shone in the prison, and he struck Peter on the side and raised him saying, "Arise quickly." And his chains fell off his hands.

The angel said, "Dress yourself and put on your sandals." He did so. Then the angel said, "Wrap your robe around you and follow me."

PETER ESCAPES

He went out and followed him. But Peter did not believe that it was true which was done by the angel, and thought he was seeing a vision.

When they had passed the first and second guard, they came to the iron gate that led into the city. It opened to them of its own accord, and they went out and passed on through one street, and then the angel departed from him.

When Peter came to himself, he said:

"Now I know as a certainty that the Lord has sent his angel and has

delivered me out of the hand of Herod, and from all that the Jewish people intended."

When he had considered this thing,

As Peter knocked at the outer doorway, a maiden named Rhoda came in answer. And when she recognized Peter's voice, her gladness was such that she did not open the gate but ran in and told the others that Peter was standing before the gate.

They said to her, "You must be mad." But she kept insisting that it was so. Then they said, "It is his angel."

Peter continued knocking, and when they had opened the door and saw him, they were astonished. But he, motioning to them with his hand to hold their peace, told them how the Lord had brought him out of the prison. And he said, "Go tell these things to the brethren." And he departed, and went to another place.

Now as soon as it was day, there was great confusion among the soldiers over what had become of Peter. And when Herod sought for him and did not find him, he questioned the guards and commanded that they should be put to death.

BARNABAS AND PAUL ARE CHOSEN

Now in the church at Antioch there were certain prophets and teachers, Barnabas, and Simeon, who was called Niger, and Lucius of Cyrene, and Manaen who had been brought up with Herod the governor, and Saul, who was also called Paul.

And as they were serving the Lord and fasting, the Holy Spirit said, "Set Barnabas and Paul apart for me for the work for which I have called them."

And when they had fasted and prayed together, and laid their hands on them, they sent them away. So Barnabas and Paul, being sent forth by the Holy Spirit, departed to Seleucia, and from there sailed to Cyprus.

he went to the house of Mary the mother of John, whose other name was Mark, where many were gathered together praying.

PAUL'S FIRST JOURNEY

 FTER preaching on the island of Cyprus, Paul and Barnabas set sail again and went to the mainland cities of Perga in Pamphylia and Antioch in Pisidia.

They were at Antioch on the sabbath day and they went into the synagogue, and sat down. And after the reading of the law and the prophets, the rulers of the synagogue sent word to them, saying, "If you have anything to preach to the people, say it."

Then Paul stood up and motioning with his hands spoke to the congregation of Jesus and the history of Israel.

"Men of Israel," he said, "and you that fear God, listen. The God of this people Israel chose our fathers and gave strength to our people when they dwelt as strangers in the land of Egypt. He delivered them with great power from their oppressors and for about forty years he maintained them in the wilderness. When he had destroyed seven nations in the land of Canaan, he divided the land to them by lot, and gave them judges for about four hundred and fifty years until Samuel the prophet.

"The people asked for a king and he gave them Saul, the son of Kish of the tribe of Benjamin for forty years. Then he raised up David in Saul's place, saying, 'I have found David the son of Jesse a man after my own heart who shall do my will.'

"Of David's seed, God according to his promises has now raised to Israel a Savior, Jesus. To you and to all who fear God is this savior and this word of salvation sent."

And the following sabbath almost the whole city came together to hear Paul and Barnabas. But their enemies stirred up the chief men of the city against them, so they departed from Antioch.

They preached in the synagogues and in the streets wherever they went, bringing the message of Jesus to Jews and Gentiles alike, for, as they said, "The Lord gave us this command: 'I have set you to be a light to the Gentiles, that you should work for the saving of souls to the ends of the earth.'"

And it came to pass in Iconium that they went together into the synagogue and spoke so that a great multitude of both the Jews and Gentiles believed. But the unbelieving Jews stirred up the Gentiles and set their minds against Paul and Barnabas. The city was divided and part held with the Jews and part with the disciples.

When an attempt was made to stone them, Paul and Barnabas were aware of it, and fled into Lystra and Derbe, other cities of Galatia, and into the region that lies round about. And there they preached the gospel.

Now there was a certain man of Lystra who, being a cripple from

PAUL'S FIRST MISSIONARY JOURNEY

birth, had never walked. He heard Paul speak, and Paul, looking at him and seeing that he had the faith to be healed, said in a loud voice, "Stand up on your feet." And he leaped up and walked.

When the people saw what Paul had done, they lifted up their voices, saying in their own tongue, "The gods have come down to us in the likeness of men." They called Barnabas Jupiter and Paul Mercury, because he was the chief speaker.

Then the priest of Jupiter, whose temple stood in front of the city, brought oxen and garlands to the gates, to offer a sacrifice with the people. And when the apostles, Paul and Barnabas, heard of this, they tore their clothes and ran among the people,

crying out, "Sirs, why do you do these things? We are only human beings, with feelings like you, and are preaching to you that you should turn from these vain worships to the living God, who made heaven and earth, and the sea, and all things in them.

"In times past he let all peoples walk in their own ways, but he did not leave us without reminders of himself, in that he did good, and gave us rain from heaven and fruitful seasons, filling our hearts with food and gladness."

Even with those words, they barely restrained the people from offering sacrifices to them.

But there came there certain men from Antioch and Iconium who swayed the people. They stoned Paul and put him out of the city, thinking he was dead. However, as the disciples stood round about him, he rose up and came into the city.

The next day, he departed with Barnabas to Derbe, and when they had preached the gospel to that city, they returned again to Lystra, and to Iconium, and Antioch.

And after they had passed throughout Pisidia, they came to Pamphylia. And when they had preached the word in Perga, they went down into Attalia, and from there sailed to Antioch in Cilicia. And there they stayed a long time with the disciples.

THE EPISTLE OF PAUL TO THE GALATIANS

Some time after leaving the Roman province of Galatia, Paul wrote a letter (epistle) to the Christian churches he had helped establish there. It is one of many he wrote to different groups. In all, the letters form a little more than a quarter of the New Testament and are full of advice and encouragement concerning Christian life and worship. Paul wrote his angry letter to the Galatians, parts of which follow, apparently after hearing of severe discord over doctrine by Galatian church members.

From Paul and all the brethren that are with me to the churches of Galatia:

"O foolish Galatians, who has bewitched you that you should not obey the truth, you before whom Jesus Christ has been clearly set forth as crucified? Only one thing would I have you tell me: Did you receive the Spirit by the works of the law or by the hearing of faith?

"Are you so foolish to believe that having begun in the Spirit, you are now made perfect by the flesh? He therefore that ministers to you the Spirit and works miracles among you, does he do it by the works of the law or by the hearing of faith?

"Be sure that they which are of faith are the children of Abraham.

"Christ has redeemed us from the curse of the law. Before faith came, we were kept under the law, shut up until faith should be revealed. The law was our schoolmaster to bring us to Christ, that we might be justified by faith. But after faith has come, we no longer need a schoolmaster.

"You are the children of God by faith in Christ Jesus. There is neither Jew nor Greek, there is neither slave nor free, there is neither male nor female, for you are all one in Jesus Christ. And if you are Christ's, then you are children of Abraham and heirs to the promises of God.

PAUL'S SECOND JOURNEY

From Antioch, Paul and Barnabas returned briefly to Jerusalem where a meeting of the apostles and many elders of the church was held to try to resolve the problem which plagued the churches of Galatia: Did Gentiles have to become Jews before they could be Christians? Paul and others persuaded, temporarily, the church leaders in Jerusalem that Gentiles could be accepted directly as Christians, as long as they followed certain minimal rules of behavior and worship.

Then Paul and Barnabas returned to Antioch and resumed teaching and preaching the word of the Lord.

FTER some days, Paul said to Barnabas, "Let us go again and visit our brethren in every city where we have preached the word of the Lord, and see how they do." But a disagreement arose between them and was so sharp that they went separate ways. Barnabas sailed to Cyprus. Paul went through Syria and Cilicia and a part of Galatia. Then after passing through Mysia, he came down to Troas.

There a vision appeared to Paul in the night. A man of Macedonia stood and begged him, saying, "Come over into Macedonia and help us." And after he had seen the vision, immediately he set out for Macedonia. From Troas, he came in a straight course to Samothrace, and the next day to Neapolis, and from there to Philippi, which was the chief city of that part of Macedonia and a Roman colony.

And it came to pass as Paul and Silas (a disciple from Jerusalem chosen by Paul to accompany him) went to pray, a certain girl possessed with a spirit of clairvoyance which brought her masters much gain met them. She followed them and cried, saying, "These men are the servants of the most high God, who tell us the way of salvation."

This she did many days. But Paul, being grieved, turned and said to the spirit, "I command you in the name of Jesus Christ to come out of her." And he came out the same hour.

And when her masters saw that the hope of their gains was gone, they caught Paul and Silas, and brought them before the rulers of the city, saying:

"These men, being Jews, do exceedingly trouble our city, and teach customs which are not lawful for us to receive, being Romans."

PAUL AND SILAS ARE IMPRISONED

And the multitude rose up together against them, and the magistrates tore off their clothing and commanded them to be beaten. And when they had laid many lashes upon them, they cast them into prison. They charged the jailer to keep them securely, and he, obeying his orders, had them thrust into the inner prison and locked their feet in the stocks.

And at midnight Paul and Silas prayed, and sang praises to God, and

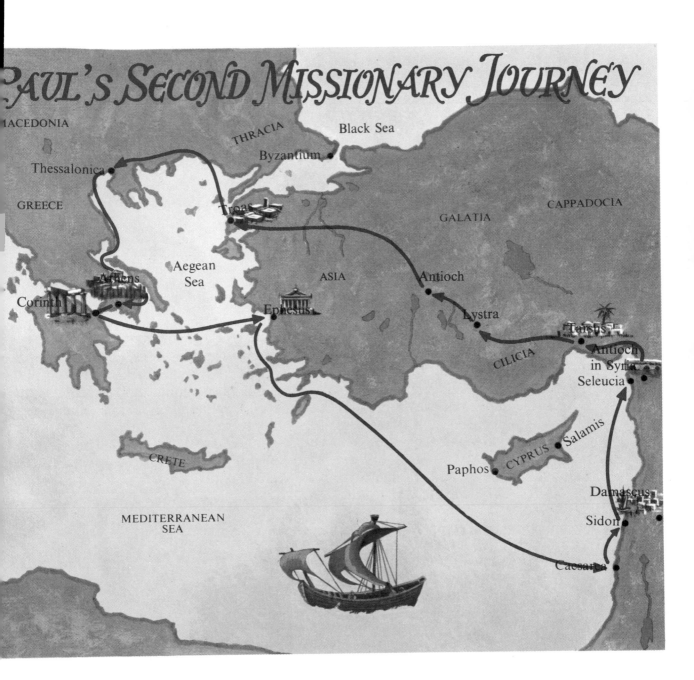

PAUL'S SECOND MISSIONARY JOURNEY

the prisoners heard them. And suddenly there was a great earthquake, so that the foundations of the prison were shaken. Immediately all the doors were opened, and everyone's bonds were loosed.

The keeper of the prison, waking out of his sleep and seeing the prison doors open, drew out his sword and would have killed himself, supposing that the prisoners had fled. But Paul cried with a loud voice, saying, "Do not harm yourself, for we are all here."

Then the jailer called for a light, and he sprang into the cell trembling, and fell down before Paul and Silas, and brought them out, and said, "Sirs, what must I do to be saved?"

And they said, "Believe in the Lord Jesus Christ, and you shall be saved, you and your house." And they spoke the word of the Lord to him, and to all that were in his house.

And the same hour of the night he took Paul and Silas and washed their wounds; and was baptized, he and all his family. And when he had brought them into his house he set meat before them, and rejoiced, believing in God with all his household.

And when it was day, the magistrates sent the sergeants, saying, "Let those men go." And the keeper of the prison told this to Paul, saying, "The magistrates have sent word to let you go. Now therefore depart and go in peace."

But Paul said, "They have beaten us openly, uncondemned, being Romans, and have cast us into prison. How do they thrust us out secretly? No indeed, let them come themselves and fetch us out."

And the sergeants told these words to the magistrates, and they feared when they heard that they were Roman citizens. And they came and begged their forgiveness, and brought them out and asked them to depart out of the city.

And they went out of the prison, and entered the house of Lydia; and when they had seen the brethren they comforted them and departed.

THEY PREACH
IN THESSALONICA

Now when they had passed through Amphipolis and Apollonia, they came to Thessalonica where there was a synagogue of the Jews. And Paul, as his manner was, went in, and on three sabbath days reasoned with them out of the scriptures, saying, "This Jesus whom I preach to you is Christ." And some of the Jews believed and joined Paul and Silas. So did a great many of the devout Greeks and not a few of the chief women.

But the Jews which did not believe, moved with envy, took certain lewd fellows of the baser sort and gathered a company and set the whole city in an uproar, crying, "These that have turned the world upside down have come here also. And these all do contrary to the decrees of Caesar, saying there is another king, one Jesus."

THEY ESCAPE FROM BEREA

And they troubled the people and the rulers of the city, when they heard these things. So the brethren immediately sent away Paul and Silas by night into Berea.

Coming there, they went into the synagogue of the Jews. These were more noble than those in Thessalonica, in that they received the word with all readiness of mind and searched the scriptures daily to find whether these things were so.

But when the Jews of Thessalonica had knowledge that the word of God was being preached by Paul at Berea, they came there also and stirred up the people. And then immediately the brethren sent Paul away toward the sea.

And they that conducted Paul brought him to Athens.

Then, after receiving for Silas and Timothy a commandment from Paul to follow him from Berea with all speed, they departed.

THE LETTERS TO THE THESSALONIANS

Arriving alone, a fugitive, in Athens, Paul must have worried about the threats to his work in the north. For, as he states in a passage from one of the two letters to the Thessalonians, he soon sent back one of his closest fellow missionaries to encourage them. That the news he received back from Thessalonica some time later was good is indicated from the two letters, parts of the first of which are given here.

"To the church of the Thessalonians: Grace be unto you, and peace, from God our Father, and the Lord Jesus Christ. We give thanks to God always for you all, making mention of you in our prayers. We remember without ceasing your work of faith and how you became followers of us and of the Lord. Having received the word in much affliction, you were examples to all that believe, in Macedonia and Achaia.

"For yourselves, brethren, know that our coming to you was not in vain. Even after we had suffered and were shamefully treated, as you know, at Philippi, our God made us bold to speak to you of his gospel in the face of much opposition.

"Then we, brothers, being taken from you—in person, not in heart—tried

733

all the more to see you again. We would have come to you—I, Paul, again and again—but Satan prevented us. Therefore we sent Timothy, our brother and minister of God and our fellow laborer in the gospel of Christ, to establish you and to comfort you concerning your faith.

"Now as touching brotherly love, you do not need me to write you, for you yourselves were taught by God to love one another—but we beseech you, brethren, that you increase in this more and more.

"But I would not have you ignorant concerning those who sleep in death, that you sorrow not like those who have no hope. For if we believe that Jesus died and rose again, so also will God bring with him those who sleep in Jesus.

"For the Lord himself shall descend from heaven with a shout, with the voice of the archangel, and with the trumpet of God. And the dead in Christ shall rise first. Then we who are alive and remain shall be caught up together with them in the clouds, to meet the Lord in the air. And so shall we ever be with the Lord. Therefore comfort one another with these words.

"The grace of our Lord Jesus Christ be with you. *Amen.*"

PAUL PREACHES TO THE ATHENIANS

Now while Paul waited for Silas and Timothy in Athens, his spirit was stirred within him when he saw the city wholly given to idolatry. Therefore he argued in the synagogue with the Jews and with the devout persons, and in the market daily with them that met with him.

Then certain philosophers of the Epicureans and of the Stoics encountered him. Some said, "What will this

babbler say?" Others said, "He seems to be a setter forth of strange gods." For he preached to them about Jesus and the resurrection.

And they took him and brought him to Areopagus, saying, "May we know what this new doctrine is of which you speak? For you are bringing strange things to our ears, and we would like to know what they mean." (For all the Athenians and strangers which were there spent their time in nothing else except telling or hearing some new thing.)

Then Paul stood in the midst of Mars' hill and said:

"You men of Athens, I see that in all things you are too superstitious. For as I passed by and beheld your devotion, I found an altar with this inscription: 'TO THE UNKNOWN GOD.' Whom therefore you worship as unknown, him shall I make known to you.

"God that made the world and all things therein, seeing that he is Lord of heaven and earth, dwells not in temples made with hands. Neither is he worshiped with men's hands, as though he needed anything, seeing that he gives to all men life and breath and all things, and has made from one blood all nations of men.

"For in him we live and move and have our being, as certain of your own poets have said, for we are his offspring. Inasmuch then as we are the offspring of God, we ought not to think that the Godhead is like gold or silver or stone or images of man's devising.

"The times of ignorance God winked at, but now he commands every man everywhere to repent, because he has appointed a day in which he will judge the world in righteousness by that man whom he has ordained. He has given assurance of that to all men by raising him from the dead."

And when they heard of the resurrection of the dead, some mocked and others said, "We will hear you again on this matter."

So Paul departed from among them. However certain men followed him and believed, among whom were Dionysius the Areopagite and a woman named Damaris, and others with them.

HE CONTINUES TO CORINTH

After these things, Paul departed from Athens and came to Corinth. And he argued in the synagogue every sabbath and persuaded the Jews and Greeks.

When Silas and Timothy arrived from Macedonia, Paul was engaged in testifying to the Jews that Jesus was Christ. And Crispus, the chief ruler of the synagogue, believed in the Lord with all his household, and many of the Corinthians hearing believed, and were baptized. And he continued there a year and six months, teaching the word of God among them.

And after this Paul took his leave of the brethren and sailed from there to Syria. And he came to Ephesus, where he entered into the synagogue and reasoned with the Jews. When they asked him to stay a longer time, he did not consent, but bade them farewell, saying, "I must by all means keep this feast that is coming in Jerusalem. But I will return again to you, if it is God's will." And he sailed from Ephesus.

THE EPISTLES OF PAUL TO THE CORINTHIANS

When Paul left Corinth, he had established there a seemingly strong and healthy following. But as he traveled, news came to him of serious conflicts within the church. These prompted his stern letters to the Corinthians, his longest writings to any one church, passages from which follow.

"To the church of God which is at Corinth: Grace be unto you, and peace, from God our Father, and from the Lord Jesus Christ.

"Now I beseech you, brethren, by the name of our Lord Jesus Christ, that you all agree and that there be no divisions among you. For it has been declared to me that there are contentions among you.

"I thank God that I baptized none of you. For Christ sent me not to baptize but to preach the gospel, not with the wisdom of words, lest the cross of Christ should lose its significance.

"For the preaching of the cross is foolishness to them that perish. But to us who are saved, it is the power of God. For it is written: 'I will destroy the wisdom of the wise, and will bring to nothing the understanding of the prudent.'

"Where is the wise? Where is the scribe? Where is the disputer of this world? Has not God made foolish the wisdom of this world? For the Jews require a sign, and the Greeks seek after wisdom. But we preach Christ crucified, a stumblingblock to the Jews and foolishness to the Greeks. But to them which are called, both Jews and Greeks, Christ is the power of God, and the wisdom of God. God has chosen the foolish things of the world to confound the wise, because the foolishness of God is wiser than men, and the weakness of God is stronger than men.

ROLE OF THE APOSTLES

"I think that God has set forth us the apostles last, as if sentenced to death. For we are made a spectacle to the world, and to angels, and to men. We are fools for Christ's sake, but you are wise in Christ. We are weak, but you are strong. You are honorable, but we are despised.

"Even to this present hour, we hunger and thirst and are naked and are buffeted and have no certain dwelling place. We labor, working with our own hands. Being reviled, we bless. Being persecuted, we bear it. Being defamed, we conciliate. We are like the filth of the world, the refuse of all things.

"I write not these things to shame you, but as my beloved sons I warn you. What will you? Shall I come to you with a rod, or in love and in the spirit of meekness?

"For to one is given by the Spirit the word of wisdom; to another the word of knowledge by the same Spirit; to another faith by the same Spirit; to another the gifts of healing by the same Spirit; to another the working of miracles; to another prophecy; to another discerning of spirits; to another divers kinds of tongues; to another the interpretation of tongues; but in all these works but one and the self-same Spirit, dividing to every man as he will.

ther we be bond or free; and have been all made to drink into one Spirit. For the body is not one member, but many. If the foot shall say, because I am not the hand I am not of the body, is it therefore not the body? And if the ear shall say, because I am not the eye I am not of the body? If the whole body were an eye, where would the hearing be? If the whole were the hearing, where would the smelling be?

"But now God has set the members, every one, in the body as it pleased him to do. And if they were all one member, where would the body be? But now they are many members, yet but one body. And the eye cannot say to the hand, I have no need of you; nor again the head to the feet, I have no need of you.

"And if one member suffers, all the members suffer with it; or if one member be honored all the members rejoice with it. Now you are the body of Christ, and members in particular. And God has set some in the church, first apostles, secondly prophets, thirdly teachers, after that miracles, then gifts of healing, helps, governments, diversities of tongues.

"Are all apostles? Are all prophets? Are all teachers? Are all workers of miracles? Have all the gift of healing? Do all speak with tongues? Do all interpret? But covet earnestly the best gifts; I will show you a more excellent way.

THE MORE EXCELLENT WAY

"Though I speak with the tongues of men and of angels, and have not love, I am become as sounding brass or a tinkling cymbal. And though I have the gift of prophecy, and the understanding of mysteries, and all knowledge; and though I have all faith, so that I could remove mountains, and

PAUL LIKENS CHRISTIANS TO THE PARTS OF A BODY

"For as the body is one, and has many members, and all the members of that one body, being many, are one body; so also is Christ. For by one Spirit are we all baptized into one body, whether we be Jew or Gentile, whehave not love, I am nothing. And though I give all my goods to feed the poor, and though my body to be burned and have not love, it profits me nothing.

Love suffers long, and is kind, love envies not; love boasts not, is not puffed up, does not behave itself unseemly, seeks not her own, is not easily provoked, thinks no evil; rejoices not in wickedness but rejoices in the truth; bears all things, believes all things, hopes all things, endures all things.

"Love never fails. But where there are prophecies, they shall fail; where there are tongues, they shall cease; where there is knowledge, it shall vanish away. For we know in part, and we prophesy in part. But when that which is perfect is come, then that which is in part shall be done away.

"When I was a child, I spoke as a child, I understood as a child, I thought as a child. But when I became a man, I put away childish things. For now we see through a glass, darkly, but then face to face. Now I know in part, but then shall I know even as also I am known.

"And now abides faith, hope, love, these three; but the greatest of these is love."

THE LETTER OF CHRIST

"Do we begin to commend ourselves again? Or do we need, as some others, epistles of commendation to you, or letters of commendation from you? You are our epistle written in our hearts, known and read by all men. For you are manifestly declared to be the epistle of Christ ministered by us, written not with ink, but with the Spirit of the living God, not in tables of stone, but in fleshy tables of the heart. Not that we are sufficient to think anything of ourselves. But our sufficiency is of God who has made us

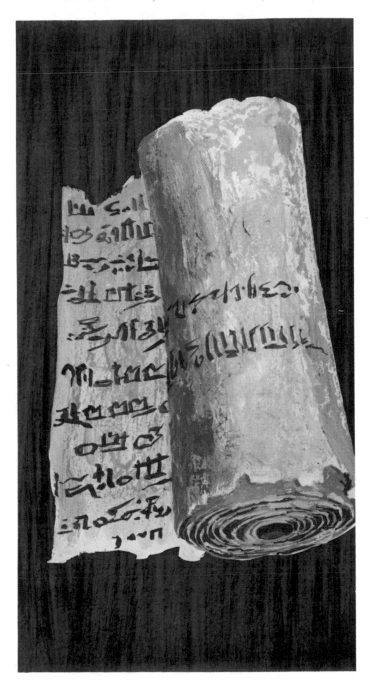

able ministers of the new testament, not of the letter, but of the spirit. For the letter kills, but the spirit gives life. Now the Lord is that Spirit, and where the Spirit of the Lord is, there is liberty."

"Finally, brethren, farewell. Be perfect, be of good comfort, be of one mind, live in peace, and the God of love and peace shall be with you."

PAUL'S THIRD JOURNEY

Sailing from Ephesus, Paul landed at Caesarea, and when he had gone up and greeted the church, he went on to Antioch. And after he had spent some time there, he departed and went over all the country of Galatia and Phrygia, strengthening all the disciples.

Then having passed through the upper coasts, Paul came again to Ephesus. And he went into the synagogue and spoke boldly for three months, disputing and persuading concerning the kingdom of God.

 OD worked special miracles through the hands of Paul, so that handkerchiefs or aprons were brought from his body to the sick, and the diseases departed from them, and the evil spirits went out of them.

Then certain vagabond Jews took it upon themselves to call the name of the Lord Jesus over those who had evil spirits, saying, "We command you by Jesus whom Paul preaches." They were seven sons of one Sceva, a Jew, and chief of the priests, who did so.

But the evil spirit answered and said, "Jesus I know, and Paul I know. But who are you?" And the man in whom the evil spirit was, leaped on them and overcame them, so that they fled naked and wounded.

This was known to all the Jews and Greeks dwelling at Ephesus, and fear fell upon them all, and the name of the Lord Jesus was praised. And many that believed came and confessed and told of their evil deeds. Many of them also who used magic brought their books together and burned them before all men. And they counted the price of them, and found it fifty thousand pieces of silver. So mightily did the word of God grow and prevail.

THE SILVERSMITHS' REVOLT

But at this time, there arose no small stir in Ephesus. For a certain man named Demetrius, a silversmith who made silver shrines for Diana, called together the workmen of like occupation and said, "Sirs, you know that by this craft we have our wealth. Moreover you see and hear that not only at Ephesus but almost throughout all Asia, this Paul has persuaded and turned away many people saying that there be no gods which are made with hands.

"So not only is our craft in danger, but also the temple of the great goddess Diana is in danger of being despised and her magnificence of being destroyed, she whom all Asia and the world worships."

When they heard these sayings, they were full of wrath and cried out, saying, "Great is Diana of the Ephesians." And the whole city was in uproar, and having caught two of Paul's companions in travel, they rushed with one accord into the theatre, where some cried one thing and some another. For the assembly was confused and most knew not why they had come together.

When the town clerk had quieted

PAUL'S THIRD MISSIONARY JOURNEY

the people, he said, "You men of Ephesus, what man is there that knows not how the city of the Ephesians is a worshiper of the great goddess Diana, and of the image which fell down from Jupiter? Seeing then that these things cannot be spoken against, you ought to be quiet and do nothing rashly. For you have brought here these men who are neither robbers of the temple nor even blasphemers of your goddess.

"Therefore if Demetrius and the craftsmen which are with him have a matter against any man, the law is open and there are deputies. Let them bring charges against one another. But if you inquire anything concerning other matters, it shall be settled in a lawful assembly. For we are in danger of being called in question for this day's uproar, there being no cause whereby we may give a justification for this meeting." And when he had thus spoken, he dismissed the assembly.

After the uproar had ceased, Paul called to him the disciples and embraced them and departed to go into Macedonia. From there he went into Greece where he stayed three months. And when his enemies laid wait for him, as he was about to sail to Syria, he returned through Macedonia instead. From there he went to Troas where he stayed for seven days.

EUTYCHUS FALLS ASLEEP

And the day before his departure, when the disciples in Troas came together for the breaking of bread, Paul preached to them, and continued talking until midnight.

There were many lights in the upper room where they were gathered together. In one window sat a certain young man named Eutychus, who had fallen into a deep sleep. As Paul was long in preaching, he sank down in his sleep and fell from the third floor, and was picked up dead.

Paul went down and threw himself upon him, and putting his arms around him, said, "Do not worry, he is still alive."

When Paul came up again, he broke bread and ate and talked a long while, until break of day, and then he departed. And they brought the young man home alive and were not a little comforted.

PAUL HASTENS TO REACH JERUSALEM

Paul hastened in order to be in Jerusalem the day of Pentecost, if it were possible. Going from Troas, he sailed from Assos, and along the coast stopped at Mitylene, Chios, Samos, Trogyllium and Miletus, then Coos, Rhodes and Patara. From there Paul and his company sailed to Syria and landed at Tyre. Next they came to Ptolemais and the following day to Caesarea.

While they were there, there came down from Judea a certain prophet named Agabus. And when he had come to them, he took Paul's girdle and bound his own hands and feet and said, "Thus says the Holy Spirit, 'So shall the Jews at Jerusalem bind the man that owns this girdle, and shall deliver him into the hands of the Gentiles.'"

When they heard these things, they begged him not to go up to Jerusalem. But Paul answered, "Why do you weep and break my heart? For I am ready not only to be bound but also to die at Jerusalem for the name of the Lord Jesus." And when he would not be persuaded, they ceased, saying, "Let the will of the Lord be done."

And after those days, they went up to Jerusalem, together with certain of the disciples of Caesarea.

PAUL IN JERUSALEM

Paul wanted very much to visit Rome, the capital of the vast empire in which he had made his missionary journeys. Looking forward to this visit, he wrote a letter to the Christian community already established and active there. He planned to make the voyage after fulfilling his mission in Jerusalem. The unhappy circumstances under which he finally did were still to be determined as he wrote this letter from Jerusalem, parts of which follow, to his distant brothers.

T O all of God's beloved in Rome called to be saints: "I make mention of you always in my prayers, requesting that by some means through the will of God I might make a journey to come to you. I long to see you to impart to you some spiritual gift, even as I have among other Gentiles. I am debtor both to the Greeks and to the Barbarians, both to the wise and to the unwise. So I am eager to preach the gospel to you that are in Rome also.

THE LOVE OF GOD

"If God be for us, who can be against us?

"Who shall separate us from the love of Christ? Shall tribulation or distress or persecution or famine or nakedness or peril or sword? As it is written, 'For thy sake we are killed all the day long. We are looked upon as sheep for slaughter.'

"No, in all these things we are more than conquerors through him that loved us. For I am persuaded that neither death, nor life, nor angels, nor principalities, nor powers, nor things present, nor things to come, nor height, nor depth, nor any other creature, shall be able to separate us from the love of God, which is in Christ Jesus our Lord.

PRAY THAT I MAY COME TO YOU

"Now, having no place more to go in these parts, and having a great desire these many years to come to you, whenever I take my journey into Spain, I will come to you.

"But now I go to Jerusalem to minister to the saints. For it has pleased them of Macedonia and Achaia to make a certain contribution for the poor saints which are at Jerusalem. When therefore I have delivered this to them, I will come by way of you to Spain.

"Now I beseech you, brethren, for the Lord Jesus Christ's sake, that you strive together in your prayers to God for me, that I may be delivered from them in Judea that do not believe and that my service which I have for Jerusalem may be accepted by the saints; that I may come to you with joy by the will of God, and may with you be refreshed. Now the God of peace be with you all. *Amen.*"

PAUL IS ARRESTED

In Jerusalem, enemies of Paul from Asia, when they saw him in the temple, stirred up all the people and seized him with great shouts, accusing him of false teaching. Then the whole city was aroused, and people hurried together, and they took Paul and dragged him out of the temple, and at once the doors were shut.

As they were about to kill him, word came to the chief captain of the soldiers that all Jerusalem was in an uproar. He immediately took soldiers and centurions and ran down to the temple. When his enemies saw the chief captain and the soldiers, they stopped beating Paul. Then the chief captain came and arrested him and commanded him to be bound with two chains, and asked who he was and what he had done.

Some cried one thing, some another, and when he could learn nothing certain because of the shouting, the captain commanded Paul to be taken into the castle. And when he came to the stairs, he had to be carried by the soldiers because of the violence of the people. For the multitude followed after, crying, "Away with him."

HE MAKES HIS DEFENSE

As Paul was being led into the castle, he said to the chief captain, "May I speak to you?" He answered, "Can you speak Greek? Are you not that Egyptian who made an uproar and led out into the wilderness four thousand men that were murderers?"

But Paul said, "I am a man who is a Jew of Tarsus, a city of Cilicia, a citizen of no mean city. I beseech you, allow me to speak to the people." And when he had given permission, Paul stood on the stairs and beckoned with his hand to the people, and when there was silence, he spoke to them in the Hebrew tongue, saying:

"Men, brethren, and fathers, hear my defense which I make now to you." When they heard that he spoke in Hebrew, they kept all the more silent. "I am truly a man who is a Jew, born in Tarsus, a city in Cilicia, yet brought up in this city at the feet of Gamaliel, and taught according to the perfect manner of the law of the fathers, and was zealous toward God, as you all are this day.

"I persecuted to death the followers of Christ, binding and delivering into prisons both men and women. As also the high priest will bear me witness, and all the elders, I received letters to the brethren, and went to Damascus to bring them which were there to Jerusalem to be punished."

Then Paul told of his conversion and baptism and his presence at Stephen's death, and how the Lord had commanded him to leave Jerusalem, saying, "Depart, for I will send you far from here, to the Gentiles."

The people listened until this word, and then they lifted up their voices and said:

"Away with such a fellow from the earth. For it is not fit that he should live."

And as they cried and cast off their clothes and threw dust into the air, the chief captain commanded him to be brought into the castle and ordered that he should be questioned by torture, so that he might know why they cried so against him.

HE PLEADS ROMAN CITIZENSHIP

As they bound him with thongs, Paul said to a centurion that stood by, "Is it lawful for you to torture a man who is a Roman, and uncondemned?"

When the centurion heard that, he went and told the chief captain, saying, "Take care in what you do, for this man is a Roman." Then the chief captain came and said to Paul, "Tell me, are you a Roman?" He said, "Yes." And the chief captain said, "For a great sum I obtained this citizenship." And Paul said, "But I was born a citizen."

And immediately, they who were to have questioned him, departed. And the chief captain was also afraid, because he knew that he was a Roman citizen and because he had bound him.

On the next day, because the chief captain wished to know why Paul was accused by his enemies, he loosed him from his bands and commanded the chief priests and all their council to appear, and brought Paul down and set him before them.

But when there arose a great dispute, the chief captain, fearing that Paul would be pulled in pieces by them, commanded the soldiers to go down and to take him by force from among them, and to bring him to the castle.

The following night, the Lord stood by him and said, "Be of good cheer, Paul. For as you have testified for me in Jerusalem, so must you bear witness also in Rome."

HIS ENEMIES PLOT
AGAINST HIM

When it was day, certain of his enemies banded together under a pledge saying that they would neither eat nor drink till they had killed Paul. They came to the chief priests and elders, and said, "Ask the chief captain to bring him down to you tomorrow, as though you wished to question him further. And we, as he comes, will be ready to kill him."

But the son of Paul's sister heard of their lying in wait and went to the castle and told Paul. Then Paul called one of the centurions and had the young man brought to the chief captain. And when he had told him of the plot, the chief captain let the young man depart, saying, "See that you tell no man that you have told these things to me."

Then he called two centurions, saying, "Make ready two hundred soldiers and go to Caesarea with seventy horsemen and two hundred spearmen. Go at the third hour of the night and bring him safe to Felix the governor."

Then the soldiers, as they were commanded, took Paul and brought him to Caesarea.

HE IS BROUGHT BEFORE FELIX

After five days, Ananias, the high priest, came down with the elders and with a certain orator named Tertullus who spoke to the governor against Paul, saying:

"We have found this man a pestilent fellow, and a mover of sedition among all the Jews throughout the world, and a ring-leader of the sect of the Nazarenes. He also has gone about profaning the temple. We seized him and would have judged him according to our law, but the chief captain came

upon us and with great violence took him away out of our hands, commanding his accusers to come to you."

Then Paul, after the governor had beckoned him to speak, answered:

"They neither found me in the temple disputing with any man, nor raising up the people in the synagogues or in the city. Nor can they prove the things of which they now accuse me."

When Felix heard these things, he said, "When the chief captain comes down, I will know more about your matter." And he commanded a centurion to guard Paul, and to let him have some liberty and that he should forbid none of his acquaintances to come to him and care for him. And Felix often sent for Paul to hear him.

Paul was still a prisoner when, after two years, Porcius Festus came to take Felix's place. And Felix, willing to do the Jews a pleasure, left Paul bound.

HE APPEALS TO CAESAR

Soon after Festus had come into the province, he commanded Paul to be brought to him as he sat on the judgment seat. And the Jews who had come down from Jerusalem laid many grievous complaints against Paul which they could not prove.

Paul answered for himself, "Neither against the law of the Jews, nor against the temple, nor yet against Caesar have I offended anything at all."

But Festus, willing to do the Jews a pleasure, asked Paul, "Are you willing to go up to Jerusalem and be judged of these things before me?"

Then Paul said, "I stand at Caesar's judgment seat, where I ought to be judged. To the Jews I have done no wrong, as you very well know. If I am an offender and have committed anything worthy of death, I do not refuse to die. But if none of these things are so, of which these men accuse me, no man may deliver me to them. I appeal to Caesar."

Then Festus, after he had conferred with the council, answered, "Have you appealed to Caesar? To Caesar you shall go."

KING AGRIPPA HEARS PAUL

Some days after, King Agrippa and his sister Bernice came to Caesarea to greet Festus. And when they had been there many days, Festus told the king about Paul's case. Then Agrippa said to Festus, "I would like to hear the man myself."

"Tomorrow," said Festus, "you shall hear him. Perhaps from your examination of him I may have something to write about him, for it seems unreasonable to send a prisoner to Rome without signifying the crimes laid against him."

The next day, in the place of hear-

ings, Paul spoke before Agrippa and Bernice and many others, explaining how he was converted and preached repentance and the way of God.

Then Agrippa said to Paul, "You almost persuade me to be a Christian."

And Paul said, "I wish to God that not only you, but also all that hear me this day, were both 'almost' and altogether like I am, except for these chains."

And when he had thus spoken, the king rose up, and the governor, and Bernice, and they that sat with them, and when they had gone aside, they talked among themselves saying, "This man has done nothing worthy of death or of chains."

Then Agrippa said to Festus, "This man might have been set at liberty if he had not appealed to Caesar."

PAUL'S JOURNEY TO ROME

HEN it was decided that Paul should sail to Italy, they delivered him and certain other prisoners to one named Julius, a centurion of Augustus's forces. Boarding a ship of Adramyttium, they launched forth, meaning to sail along the coast of Asia.

The next day, they touched at Sidon and Julius courteously gave Paul liberty to go to his friends to refresh himself.

When they left there, they sailed along the coast of Cyprus, because the winds were contrary. They came to Myra, a city of Lycia, where the centurion found a ship from Alexandria sailing to Italy, and he put his prisoners on it.

When they had sailed slowly many days, without favorable winds, they came to a place which is called 'The Fair Havens,' near the city of Lasea. Much time had passed and seafaring was now dangerous, for the winter had nearly come.

Paul warned them, "Sirs, I foresee that this voyage will bring damage and loss, not only of the cargo and ship, but also of our lives."

Nevertheless the centurion believed the captain and the owner of the ship more than Paul. And because the harbor was not well suited to winter in, most people advised departure, in order, if it were at all possible, to reach Phoenix, which is a harbor of Crete, and winter there.

When the south wind blew softly, thinking that they could reach their goal, they untied and set sail close to Crete. But very soon there arose a mighty gale. The ship was caught and could not face into the wind, so they let it run before it.

And running behind a small island called Clauda, they had much work in making fast the ship's boat. When the boat had been taken up, they ran ropes under the ship to secure it. Then, fearing that they might run onto the sand, they struck the sails and let the ship drift.

Being greatly tossed about by the tempest, the next day they lightened the ship. And the following day with their own hands, they threw out the ship's tackle. But when neither sun nor stars appeared for many days, and the great storm still raged, all hope of being saved was given up.

But after going without food for a long time, Paul stood up in the midst of them and said, "Sirs, you should have listened to me and not have loosed from Crete. But now I exhort you to be of good cheer, for there shall be no loss of any man's life among you, but only the ship. For there stood by me this night the angel of God, whose I am and whom I serve, saying, 'Fear not, Paul. You must be brought before Caesar, and, lo, God has put under your protection all them that sail with you.' Therefore, sirs, be of good cheer. For I believe God, that it shall be even as it was told me. However, we must be cast upon a certain island."

THE SHIP RUNS AGROUND

When the fourteenth night had come, about midnight the men of the ship felt that they were drawing near to land. They took soundings and then cast four anchors off the stern. When they had let down the boat, about to flee the ship, Paul said to the centurion and to the soldiers, "Unless these men stay with the ship, you cannot be saved." Then the soldiers cut the ropes of the boat, and let her drift away.

While the day was coming on, Paul asked them all to take food, saying,

"This day is the fourteenth day that you have taken nothing. Therefore I pray you to eat, for this is for your health. For not a hair shall fall from the head of any of you."

And when he had thus spoken, he took bread and gave thanks to God, and when he had broken it, he began to eat. Then they were all of good cheer, and they also took some food. And they were in all two hundred and seventy-six souls on the ship.

When they had eaten enough, they lightened the ship, casting out the cargo of wheat into the sea. And when it was day, the land was unknown to them, from their plan, and commanded that those who could swim should cast themselves first into the sea and get to land; then the rest should follow, some on boards and some on broken pieces of the ship. And it came to pass that they all escaped safe to land.

THEY WINTER ON MALTA

After their escape, they found that the island was called Melita (Malta). The natives there showed them much kindness, for they kindled a fire and welcomed them all to it, because of the rain and the cold.

When Paul had gathered a bundle of sticks and laid them on the fire, a viper came out because of the heat and fastened itself on his hand.

When the natives saw the poisonous beast hang from his hand, they said among themselves, "No doubt this man is a murderer whom justice will not permit to live, although he has escaped the sea."

But Paul shook the beast off into the fire and felt no harm. They looked for him to swell or fall down dead suddenly, but after they had looked a great while, and saw no harm come to him, they changed their minds and said that he was a god.

Now in the same area were the lands of the chief man of the island, whose name was Publius. He welcomed Paul and lodged him courteously for three days. The father of Publius lay sick with a fever and a flow of blood and Paul prayed and healed him. So when this was done, others on the island which had diseases came and were healed. They heaped honors on Paul, and when he departed, they gave him all he needed.

After three months, he left in a ship from Alexandria which had wintered at the island. He went to Syracuse, to Rhegium, to Puteoli and so to Rome.

but they saw a creek with a beach where they planned, if it were possible, to run the ship ashore. So they took up the anchors, loosed the rudder bands, and hoisted the mainsail to the wind and, committing themselves to the sea, made toward shore.

And falling onto a shoal, they ran the ship aground. The forepart stuck fast and remained unmovable, but the after part was broken with the violence of the waves.

Now the soldiers' plan was to kill the prisoners lest any of them should swim out and escape. But the centurion, wanting to save Paul, kept them

PAUL'S FINAL YEARS

When they had appointed him a day, there came many to him in his lodging. From morning till evening, he talked to them about the kingdom of God, persuading them concerning Jesus. And some believed the things which were spoken, and some believed not. And when they did not agree among themselves, Paul said, "Well spoke the Holy Spirit through Isaiah the prophet to our fathers, saying: 'Hearing you shall hear, and shall not understand: and seeing you shall see, and not perceive. For the heart of this people has become heavy, and their ears are dull of hearing, and their eyes they have closed.'

HEN the brethren in Rome heard of Paul's arrival, they came to meet him as he approached, going as far as the Appian Forum and The Three Taverns. And when Paul saw them, he thanked God, and took courage.

And when he came to Rome, the centurion delivered the prisoners to the captain of the guard. But Paul was allowed to dwell by himself with a soldier to guard him.

After three days, Paul called the chiefs of the Jews together, and said to them, "Men and brethren, though I have committed nothing against the people or customs of our fathers, yet I was delivered prisoner from Jerusalem into the hands of the Romans."

They said to him, "We neither received letters from Judea concerning you, nor have any of the brethren that came spoken any harm of you. But we desire to hear what you think. For as concerning this sect, we know that everywhere it is spoken against."

"Be it known therefore to you that the salvation of God has been sent to the Gentiles, and they will hear it." And when he had said these words, the Jews departed and had great disputing among themselves.

And Paul dwelt two whole years in his own rented house, and received all that came to him, preaching the kingdom of God and teaching those things which concern the Lord Jesus, with all confidence, no man forbidding him.

THE LETTERS FROM ROME

During his long semi-confinement in Rome, Paul wrote to many groups and individuals, his letters making up some of the final chapters of the New Testament. Like his earlier epistles, these are full of spiritual advice from which many of the basic elements of Christian belief have been drawn. Some selected passages are given here with the name of the group or person to whom they were written.

OF THE ARMOR OF FAITH
(FROM EPHESIANS)

"Be strong in the Lord, and in the power of his might. Put on the whole armor of God, that you may be able to stand against the wiles of the devil. For we wrestle not against flesh and blood, but against principalities, against powers, against the rulers of the darkness of this world, against spiritual wickedness in high places.

"Stand therefore having your loins wrapped around with truth, and having on the breastplate of righteousness. Have your feet shod with the preparation of the gospel of peace. Above all, take the shield of faith, with which you shall be able to quench all the fiery darts of the wicked. And take the helmet of salvation, and the sword of the Spirit, which is the word of God."

THINK ABOUT THESE THINGS
(FROM PHILIPPIANS)

"Brethren, whatever things are true, whatever things are honest, whatever things are just, whatever things are pure, whatever things are lovely, whatever things are of good report, and if there be any virtue and if there be any praise, think about these things. Those things which you have both learned and received and heard and seen in me, do; and the God of peace shall be with you."

SEEK THOSE THINGS WHICH ARE ABOVE
(FROM COLOSSIANS)

"If you have been raised with Christ, seek those things which are above, where Christ sits on the right hand of God. Set your affection on things above, not on things on earth."

In a short letter to Philemon, an old friend of Paul's and a leader of the Colossian Christians, Paul asks him to receive back a runaway slave whom he has converted.

(FROM PHILEMON)

"For, perhaps, he departed for a season so that you should receive him for ever. Not now as a servant, but above a servant, as a beloved brother. If you consider me therefore a partner, receive him as myself. If he wronged you or owes you anything, put that on my account. I Paul have written it with my own hand; I will repay it."

OF FAITH WITHOUT WAVERING
(FROM HEBREWS)

"Let us hold fast the profession of our faith without wavering, for he is faithful that promised: 'The just shall live by faith, but if any man shrinks back, my soul shall have no pleasure in him.'

"Now faith is the substance of things

hoped for, the evidence of things not seen. Through faith we understand that the worlds were framed by the word of God, so that things which are seen were made out of things which do not appear."

(FROM II TIMOTHY)

What happened to Paul after his two years in Rome is not certain. The Bible leaves off with him awaiting trial. Some scholars believe he was released and left Rome. But traditionally it is held that he was still there during Nero's persecution of Christians and that he was beheaded after being heard and sentenced by Nero himself.

In any case, among his very last writings must be counted his second epistle to Timothy. In this letter to his long faithful lieutenant, he talks of his death as an approaching certainty.

"I am now ready to be offered, and the time of my departure is at hand. I have fought a good fight, I have finished my course, I have kept the faith. Henceforth there is laid up for me a crown of righteousness, which the Lord, the righteous judge, shall give me on the day of judgment. And not only to me, but to all them also that love his appearing.

"Do your best to come to me shortly. The others have deserted me. Only Luke is with me. Take Mark and bring him with you, for he is profitable to me for the ministry. The cloak that I left at Troas with Carpus, when you come, bring it with you, and the books, especially the parchments.

"The Lord Jesus Christ be with your spirit. Grace be with you. *Amen.*"

from I PETER and II PETER

THE LETTERS OF PETER

The later pages of the New Testament were written during the years of widespread persecution of early Christians by the Romans. They point to future glory as the reward for present suffering and warn against spiritual weakness. These pages, which follow the epistles of Paul, comprise letters by four other leaders of the growing church, among them Simon Peter, the apostle of Christ.

OW who is he that will harm you, if you are followers of that which is good? But even if you suffer for righteousness' sake, happy are you. And be not afraid of terror, nor be troubled. For it is better, if the will of God be so, that you suffer for well doing than for evil doing. For Christ also once suffered for sins, the just for the unjust, that he might bring us to God, being put to death in the flesh but made alive in the Spirit."

PETER COUNSELS HUMILITY

"All of you be subject to one another, and be clothed with humility. For God resists the proud and gives grace to the humble. Humble yourselves therefore under the mighty hand of God, that he may exalt you in due time. Cast all your care upon him, for he cares for you.

"Be sober, be vigilant, because your adversary the devil, like a roaring lion, walks about, seeking whom he may devour. Resist him, steadfast in the faith, knowing that the same sufferings are befalling your brothers throughout the world."

PETER SPEAKS OF THE COMING OF THE LORD

"But, beloved, be not ignorant of this one thing, that one day is with the Lord as a thousand years, and a thousand years as one day. The Lord is not slack concerning his promise, as some men count slackness, but is long-suffering, not willing that any should perish, but that all should come to repentance.

"But the day of the Lord shall come like a thief in the night, in which the heavens shall pass away with a great noise, and the elements shall melt with burning heat. The earth also and the works that are on it shall be burned up. Nevertheless we, according to his promise, look for new heavens and a new earth, where righteousness will dwell.

"Therefore, beloved, seeing that you look for such things, be careful that you be found by him in peace, without spot, and blameless. And count the long-suffering of our Lord as salvation, as our beloved brother Paul has written to you, speaking of these things in all his epistles.

"Grow in grace and in the knowledge of our Lord and Savior Jesus Christ."

from the
BOOK OF REVELATION

THE VISION
OF JOHN

The final book of the Bible, The Revelation of St. John the Divine, tells in vivid images of God's final judgment.

The book is cast in the form of a vision and many of its prophecies are disguised attacks on Rome, the great power of the first century. Such is unquestionably the case of the references to Babylon. This ancient capital of paganism and persecution was comparable in the eyes of early Christians to the Rome of their day. Thus the following passages must have been clear and encouraging to many.

"And after these things, I saw another angel come down from heaven, having great power. And he cried mightily with a strong voice, saying, 'Babylon the great has fallen, and is become the habitation of devils and the hold of every foul spirit, and a cage of every unclean and hateful bird.'

"And I heard another voice from heaven, saying, 'Come out of her, my people, that you be not partakers of her sins, and that you receive not her plagues. For her sins have reached into heaven, and God has remembered her iniquities.

"'And the kings of the earth, when they shall see the smoke of her burning, standing afar off for the fear of her torment, shall say, "Alas, alas, that great city Babylon, that mighty city."'"

A NEW HEAVEN AND EARTH

"And I saw a new heaven and a new earth, for the first heaven and the first earth had passed away, and there was no more sea. And I, John, saw the holy city, new Jerusalem, coming down from God out of heaven, prepared as a bride adorned for her husband.

"And I heard a great voice out of heaven, saying, 'Behold, the tabernacle of God is with men, and he will dwell with them, and they shall be his people. And he shall wipe away all tears from their eyes, and there shall be no more death, nor sorrow, nor crying. Neither shall there be any more pain.'

"And he carried me away in the spirit to a great and high mountain, and showed me that great city, the holy Jerusalem. And her light was like a stone most precious, even like a jasper stone, clear as crystal. And she had a wall great and high, and had twelve gates. The wall of the city had twelve foundations, and in them the names of the twelve apostles of the Lamb.

"And I saw no temple therein, for the Lord God Almighty and the Lamb are the temple of it. And the city had no need of the sun, nor of the moon, to shine in it. For the glory of God did lighten it, and the Lamb is the light thereof.

"And the nations of them which are saved shall walk in the light of it, and the kings of the earth bring their glory and honor to it. And the gates of it shall not be shut at all by day, for there shall be no night there.

"And I, John, saw these things, and heard them."

INDEX